Contents

What is air?

Air is what we breathe to stay alive. It is all around you, but you cannot see or smell it. You cannot touch it, but you can feel it when the wind blows, or when you blow on your skin.

❯❯ You can give shape to the air by blowing bubbles. The soap traps the air to make bubbles.

Our Earth

The Air we Breathe

Jen Green

First published in 2007 by Wayland

This paperback edition published
in 2011 by Wayland

Copyright © Wayland 2007

Wayland
338 Euston Road
London NW1 3BH

Wayland Australia
Level 17/207 Kent Street
Sydney NSW 2000

Produced by Tall Tree Ltd
Editor: Jon Richards
Designer: Ben Ruocco
Consultant: John Williams

British Library Cataloguing in Publication
Data
  Green, Jen
  The air we breathe. - (Our Earth)
  1. Atmosphere - Juvenile literature
  I. Title
  551.5'1

ISBN 9780750265126

Printed in China
Wayland is a division of Hachette
Children's Books, an Hachette UK Company.
www.hachette.co.uk

Picture credits:
Cover Dreamstime.com/Jens Mayer,
1 Dreamstime.com/Mike Schrengohst,
4 Dreamstime.com/Charles Shapiro,
5 Dreamstime.com/Monika Wisniewska,
6 Dreamstime.com/Mike Mu, 7 NASA
8 Dreamstime.com/Elena Elisseeva,
9 Alamy/Jake Norton,
10 Dreamstime.com/Marilyn Barbone,
11 Dreamstime.com/Mike Schrengohst,
12 Dreamstime.com/Hermann Danzmayr,
13 Dreamstime.com/Nick Stubbs,
14 Dreamstime.com/Alon Othnay,
15 Dreamstime.com/Iryna Shpulak,
16 Dreamstime.com/Jens Mayer,
17 Dreamstime.com/Anthony Hathaway,
18 Corbis/Fabio Cardoso/zefa,
19 Dreamstime.com/Brett Atkins,
20 Digital Vision, 21 Tall Tree Ltd

All animals, including dogs and humans, need oxygen for energy.

Air is a mixture of gases, including **oxygen**. Oxygen is vital to living things on Earth. People need to breathe oxygen every minute of every day to stay alive.

The atmosphere

Air forms a layer around the Earth called the **atmosphere**. The atmosphere acts like a blanket. It keeps the Earth warm and makes it a comfortable place to live.

⬇ If the Earth was the same size as an orange, the atmosphere would be a similar thickness to the skin.

This picture taken from a
satellite in space shows the
atmosphere as a blue haze
above the Earth's surface.

The atmosphere contains several layers,
one on top of the other. Each layer
contains less air than the one below it.
The top layer fades off into space.

Air pressure

Even though you do not feel it, air has weight. It presses on everything beneath it. This is called **air pressure**.

At **sea level**, air pressure is high and there is enough oxygen for us to breathe normally.

Fact

The air at the top of the world's highest mountain is only about one-third as thick as air at sea level.

Close to the Earth's surface, there is a lot of air pushing down so air pressure is at its highest here. On the highest mountains, there is very little air pushing down, so air pressure is lower than at sea level.

⛰ On the highest mountains, there is not enough oxygen for us to breathe normally. Climbers carry bottles of oxygen to survive.

Rising and sinking air

When the sun shines, it warms the ground, which warms the air above it. As the air gets warm, it rises. This causes **currents** of rising air, called **thermals**.

❯❯ Birds such as eagles and kites use thermals to stay in the air without flapping their wings.

Hot-air balloons warm the air inside the balloons with burners. This warm air lifts the balloons off the ground.

As the air rises, it moves away from the warm ground and starts to cool. As the air cools, it **contracts** and becomes heavier and sinks back down to the ground again.

Fact

The Montgolfier brothers of France made the first balloon flight in 1783.

Moving air

Wind is air moving from one place to another. When warm air rises, cooler air rushes in to replace it. The rushing air is a wind.

This wind sock shows people how strong the wind is.

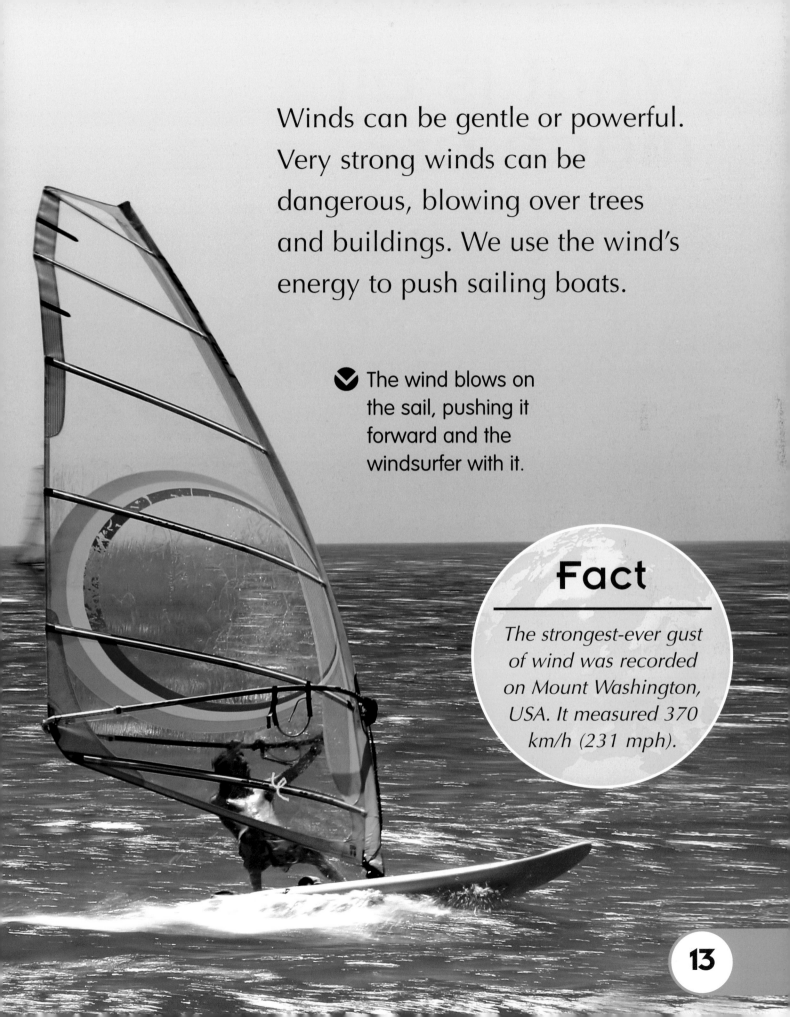

Winds can be gentle or powerful. Very strong winds can be dangerous, blowing over trees and buildings. We use the wind's energy to push sailing boats.

⌄ The wind blows on the sail, pushing it forward and the windsurfer with it.

Fact

The strongest-ever gust of wind was recorded on Mount Washington, USA. It measured 370 km/h (231 mph).

What is air made of?

Most of the air we breathe is made up of oxygen and nitrogen. There are also small amounts of other gases. These include **carbon dioxide** which is very important to plants.

▼ The sky is blue because the gases in the air make that colour.

Air also contains water in the form of a gas called **water vapour**. You can see water in the air when tiny water droplets gather to form clouds.

Rain falls when water droplets in clouds bump together and get so heavy that they fall to the ground.

The Earth's gases

Plants add oxygen to the atmosphere. They take carbon dioxide from the air and use it to grow. They give off oxygen, which animals, including people, need to breathe.

⊽ Plants use energy from sunlight, carbon dioxide and water to make their own food.

⬧ Winds spread oxygen around the world, so animals in every place on Earth can breathe, including polar bears in the North Pole.

As animals breathe, they use up oxygen, and breathe out carbon dioxide. In this way, plants and animals help to **maintain** the balance of gases in the air.

Oxygen for life

People breathe using their lungs. When you breathe in, air enters your lungs. Oxygen passes into your blood and is pumped around your body by your heart.

⬆ We cannot get oxygen from water. Instead, we have to take a big breath before diving underwater.

All animals need oxygen to live, but some do not need to breathe air. Fish get the oxygen they need directly from the water they swim in, rather than by breathing air.

⊻ Whales need to breathe air, like us. They regularly come to the surface to breathe.

19

Keeping the air clean

Living things need clean air to breathe. If they breathe in dirty air, then there is less oxygen in it or there might be chemicals that could make people ill.

⊗ Factories and cars pump smoke and chemicals into the air. This is called **pollution**.

⬆ You can reduce pollution by
taking the bus to school
instead of going by car.

Fact

A dirty haze called
smog hangs over some
large cities. It is caused
by pollution from cars
and factories.

Factories, cars and homes burn **fuel** to
produce energy. When they burn fuel, they
release pollution into the air. We can all
help to keep the air clean by using less
energy. Switch off lights and other
machines when you are not using them.

Activities

Make a parachute

Parachutes slow the fall of something through the air. See how the size of a parachute can affect its speed.

WHAT YOU NEED

- Plastic bag cut into different sized squares
- String
- Sticky tape
- Metal washers

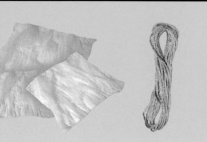

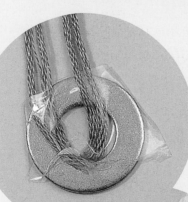

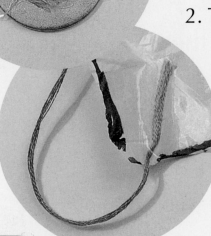

1. Cut four pieces of string, all the same length. Tape one end of each piece of string to a washer.
2. Tape the other ends to a corner of the smallest piece of plastic.
3. Repeat these stages, using a larger piece of plastic.
4. Drop the parachutes from the same height at the same time. You will see that the larger parachute takes longer to fall.

Weighing air

Although you do not feel it, air actually has weight. This project will show you how you can compare the different weights of different amounts of air.

WHAT YOU NEED

- Stick
- String
- Three balloons
- Scissors

40 cm

1. Cut three equal lengths of string. Tie one piece of string to the middle of the stick and the other two pieces to either end.

2. Blow up two of the balloons so that they are the same size. Now tie each balloon to either end of the stick. Because they hold the same amount of air, they weigh the same and the stick will stay level.

3. Blow up the third balloon, but with less air. Now tie it to one end of the stick, replacing one of the first pair of balloons. Does the stick stay level?

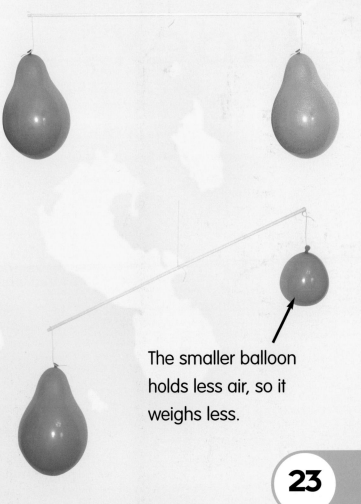

The smaller balloon holds less air, so it weighs less.

Glossary

Air pressure The force of the atmosphere pressing down on the Earth.

Atmosphere The layer of gases which surrounds the Earth.

Carbon dioxide A gas used by plants to make their food, and which animals release into the air as they breathe.

Contracts When something gets smaller.

Currents Movements of air or water across the Earth's surface.

Fuel Something that we burn to produce light and heat.

Maintain To keep something the same.

Nitrogen The main gas in the air. It makes up about four-fifths of the atmosphere.

Oxygen A gas in the air, which is vital to life on Earth. It makes up just less than one-fifth of the atmosphere.

Pollution Any solid, liquid or gas that causes harm to nature. Pollution is given off by factories, cars, power stations and our homes.

Sea level The height at which the sea sits.

Smog A dark, smoky haze that is usually produced by pollution.

Thermals Currents of warm, rising air.

Water vapour Water in the form of a gas.

Index